HOBBIES YOU ENJOY

HOUSE OF VLAD

BRIAN ALAN ELLIS, owner and founder of House of Vlad Press and *Vlad Mag*, has published several books. His writing has appeared at *Juked*, *Hobart*, *Monkeybicycle*, *Fanzine*, *Electric Literature*, *Vol. 1 Brooklyn*, *X-R-A-Y*, *Heavy Feather Review*, *HAD*, *BULL* and *Forever Magazine*, among many other places. He lives in Florida.

HOBBIES YOU ENJOY

A NOVELTY

BRIAN ALAN ELLIS

A HOUSE OF VLAD PRODUCTION
© 2026, © 2025, © 2024 by Brian Alan Ellis

Printed in Super Fun Land, USA

A version of *Hobbies You Enjoy: A Novelty* was originally serialized on Instagram, 2021-2023.

The author wishes to thank Garielle Lutz for her editing suggestions.

Book design: Percy Hearst
Photos © Brian Alan Ellis

HOUSEOFVLADPRESS.COM

ISBN: 9798390308127

For longing and dread

IN MEMORY OF GIAN

"yeah pretty sure i want this man...
gonna print this out this week
and start going through it.
I like what youve done with it so far"

— Giancarlo DiTrapano,
from an email to the author
(Mon, Feb 22, 2021, 4:55 AM)

WARNING

There is little-to-no plot or character development in this book. If you feel like you've been cheated, you have. Reader discretion is advised.

"The only insult I've ever received in my adult life was when someone asked me, 'Do you have a hobby?' A HOBBY?! DO I LOOK LIKE A FUCKING DABBLER?!"

JOHN WATERS

HOBBIES YOU ENJOY

WHAT IS THAT?
St. Jude Children's
Research Hospital

BENOIT LELIEVRE

Dead End Follies
(2024)

Today you swiped up, up, down, down, left, right, left right, b, a, start on your co-worker's Tinder when he wasn't looking.

Every author has an unspoken (or outspoken) desire to make people cry. Because tears are considered hard evidence of a meaningful emotional connection and it's really difficult to pull off with written words. But those who achieve such a connection all share a similar trait: extreme, boundless authenticity. They're pathologically themselves and let their work resonate with whoever might feel compelled. Not everyone will see the beauty in Brian Alan Ellis's meta-ironic shitposting, but I sure do and I will always advocate it.

His new novel / journal / whatever-it-is, *Hobbies You Enjoy*, is upon us and he's refined the art of being so unapologetically himself again.

So, *Hobbies You Enjoy* is a 365-day journal where the narrator (it might be Brian Alan Ellis himself, I was never sure) describes what he did to entertain himself. All the entries begin with the words "Today you..." and last no more than four or five lines each. They range from interactions with mundane pop culture to invocation of nostalgic memories via weekly psychological breakdowns. In trademark Brian Alan Ellis fashion, it's both absurdly easy to read and low-key complex and emotionally charged.

DISTRACTION IS DEPRESSION

Hobbies You Enjoy is obviously mocking the idea of gratitude journaling, a self-help practice meant to rewire your brain to appreciate what you have instead of longing for what you lost. But instead of firing on all cylinders and being obvious as shit, Ellis takes the smart route. He traces a portrait of how hollow the cultural devices you're supposed to fill your life with really are. Whether it's social media, dating apps, television, alcohol, music, the journal entries explore how they don't have the power to change you.

> Today someone, after noticing you contemplating their Grateful Dead t-shirt, asked if you were a Deadhead, and you said no, that you're more of a "grateful to actually *be* dead" type, and the person said, "Oh, so like a goth?"

When the narrator is actually interacting with someone, popular culture (as exemplified above) serves to separate people, not unify them like it's been championed to. Everyone is trapped in their own algorithmically made journey of meaning and solitude. No one has the same tastes, so no one has the same experiences. So, the narrator turns to old artifacts of monoculture like ALF or old school wrestling in order to sense a connection, only to realize no one remembers this at all but him.

Hobbies You Enjoy is obviously a tweak on an established formula for Brian Alan Ellis, but it's his most vibrant yet, and to my knowledge, his book that acknowledges aging from the perspective of someone who spent a life distracting himself from deeply rooted issues that he neither had the money or support to challenge on his own terms. It's as witty and tongue-in-cheek as anything Ellis has ever done, but it comes from a much more personal and wounded place than the depression memes you can find online.

THE ART OF KEEPING INVISIBLE WOUNDS INVISIBLE

What I find so moving about Brian Alan Ellis's work is that they're an everyday (literally in *Hobbies You Enjoy*) manifestation of unspoken, invisible wounds that even the wounded person feeling them might not fully understand. Ellis's work is self-aware by nature, but there's an inherent suffering to his brand of nostalgia that charges it with an emotional added value if you're old enough to understand what the fuck he's actually talking about. Instead of longing for the past, he's trying to numb this goddamned self-awareness.

> Today you reminisced about a lost Polaroid from 1989, where an eight-year-old version of you is posing with the saddest guy in a Batman costume you'd ever seen while at a comic bookstore in an outlet mall on Long Island.

The tragedy of Ellis's writing is that this self-awareness chases him everywhere and taints what little of an innocence he once had. His present is poisoning the little bliss he's had as a kid, but that bliss is also alleviating the effect of the poisonous lifestyle he's living now. If that isn't relatable to you, you're either extremely privileged or extremely oppressed. If the idea of ordinary suffering, of invisible wounds, is alien to you, or you haven't come to terms with your own bullshit, you're honestly missing out.

If you're familiar with Brian Alan Ellis's writing, *Hobbies You Enjoy* is not going to blow you out of the water. It's basically a sharper, more emotionally attuned version of what he's always done. But Ellis is original and reliable, like a death metal band that understands its audience. He's also unapologetically brave and vulnerable despite being ironic. That's what makes him so relatable to me. Reading about a guy facing his demons in such a blunt and graceful way inspires me to be more courageous against my own.

PROLOGUE

— 31 —

Today you made a contribution to the arts by wandering aimlessly around town in a sad, drunken stupor.

JANUARY

— 1 —

Today you woke up to a series of texts telling you that you are "nasty and vindictive" and that you "suffocate people," which means "Happy New Year."

— 2 —

Today you remembered that having hobbies and/or passions has pretty much ruined your life.

— 3 —

Today you tossed all your bright ideas into a burning pile of previous bright ideas.

— 4 —

Today you contemplated important life decisions while staring dead-eyed into the 7-Eleven hot bar.

— 5 —

Today you repeatedly logged on to various social media accounts, each time expecting different results.

— 6 —

Today you hyperventilated into a limited-edition ALF hand puppet purchased from Burger King in 1988.

— 7 —

Today you listlessly tormented your cat with an empty Pringles can.

$$-8-$$

Today you considered launching a Kickstarter campaign to help fund a line of nihilistic teddy bears for kids (Un-BEARables™) that you hope to one day manufacture and sell while laughing maniacally like an evil genius looking to destroy the world one morally corrupted child at a time.

$$-9-$$

Today you realized that living alone has afforded you the luxury to finally spread your depression throughout an entire enclosure without bumming anyone else out.

$$-10-$$

Today, having been productive in very short bursts, you rewarded yourself by staring blankly into nothingness for what seemed like a long, long time.

Today, browsing the $5 DVD bin at Walmart, you imagined strangers cheering you on as they held your legs like you were doing a keg stand.

Today, to help mask the pain, you wore some "fly-ass gear" purchased via targeted ads on your Facebook timeline.

Today you pictured what it would look like to have the saddest piss in a pissing contest.

Today you spiritually identified as the last sip of soda used to extinguish cigarettes dropped inside of a 20 oz. Diet Dr Pepper bottle.

Today you gave someone good advice while making your own bad decisions.

Today you imagined yourself falling down the stairs while wearing a t-shirt that had "The Dream Died" (or "Dream's Dead") (or "Dreams R.I.P.") printed on it.

— 17 —

Today, instead of counting sheep, you fell asleep by ranking the many panic attacks you'd had earlier.

— 18 —

Today you got "lit" on 2-liter bottles of Mountain Dew Livewire while watching documentaries about serial killers for what seemed like a long, long time.

— 19 —

Today you googled "most fly-ass gear millennials should wear when roundhouse kicking people in the face à la Chuck Norris," which resulted in slight disappointment.

— 20 —

Today you had a very disturbing wet dream about being mauled by dogs at a Toys"R"Us.

— 21 —

Today you admitted to someone that not having an actual father is the reason you read daily horoscopes while sitting alone at the bar.

— 22 —

Today, after going into detail about that curious warmth you'd feel as a teenager whenever your player in *NBA Jam* would shatter the digital backboard, you skillfully side-stepped the inevitable "Do you play video games?" question asked by every stoned twenty-something-year-old you're expected to train while at work.

— 23 —

Today you said, "Hey, no worries," while also thinking, *Ohhh Fuuuuck!*

— 24 —

Today you tried convincing someone that LinkedIn is actually an elaborate joke orchestrated by hipsters.

— 25 —

Today you tried endorsing someone on LinkedIn for being skilled at "narcissistic crying while spiritually drowning in the muck of life."

— 26 —

Today you wrote "Slim Shady" on one of those HELLO MY NAME IS stickers, which resulted in slight disappointment.

— 27 —

Today you sexually identified as an "Out of Order" sign Scotch-taped to the door of a bathroom stall.

— 28 —

Today you woke up, hungover and death-ready, to the memory of your stepdad shaming you for skipping school and going to see the 1999 *South Park* movie on the same day your mom had cancer-related surgery.

— 29 —

Today you renamed your cat PUNK HOUSE.

— 30 —

Today your inner child was fucked up on whippets.

— 31 —

Today you remembered that it just keeps getting worse.

FEBRUARY

— 1 —

Today you sexually identified as a cell phone someone had accidentally dropped into a toilet.

— 2 —

Today you tried recklessly obliterating all your ex's mixed signals like they were targets in a next-gen shooter a neck-bearded incel would play in their mom's basement.

— 3 —

Today you considered launching a Kickstarter campaign to help fund a dating site for plus-sized goths (Funeral Fatties dot com) that you hope to one day pitch on an episode of *Shark Tank*.

— 4 —

Today you considered holding a clipboard in a very professional manner while asking random couples entering an Olive Garden whether they'd rather fuck inside of a Dollar Tree, a Dollar General, or a Family Dollar.

— 5 —

Today you devised wild scenarios and alternative endings to season three of *Rock of Love with Bret Michaels,* which first aired several years ago.

— 6 —

Today you fantasized about being held—forcibly underwater until your lungs filled and you drowned.

— 7 —

Today you nurtured your crippling intimacy issues by preparing and then eating one fried bologna sandwich at a time.

— 8 —

Today you remembered that love can't fix whatever is wrong with you and that you'll probably one day get blackout drunk before using the inside of your hypothetical partner's vehicle as a toilet.

— 9 —

Today you pictured yourself double-fisting longing and dread at "tha club."

— 10 —

Today you contemplated the alarming lack of character development in all seven *Police Academy* films.

Today, after revisiting all seven *Police Academy* films, you realized that Bobcat Goldthwait's character, "Zed," is the most developed of the bunch; throughout the three *Police Academy* films he's in, Goldthwait's "Zed" leaves a life of crime to become a cop and then falls in love.

Today you ruined a potential relationship by being hung up on the ghosts of previous relationships.

Today you imagined having existential black holes in different area codes.

— 14 —

Today you fantasized about all the different texts your ex could send to make you feel loved and less alone but won't.

— 15 —

Today you lingered over a co-worker's shoulder as he navigated his Tinder for what seemed like a long, long time.

— 16 —

Today you swiped up, up, down, down, left, right, left, right, b, a, start on your co-worker's Tinder when he wasn't looking.

— 17 —

Today you tried convincing someone that it's best to just showcase your worst qualities to people, especially if those qualities include owning entire seasons of Criss Angel's *Mindfreak* on DVD.

— 18 —

Today you snorted drugs off the spare house key you still haven't given back to your ex.

— 19 —

Today you wished that bad relationships were tax deductible.

— 20 —

Today, while in the mood for some real shenanigans, you searched YouTube for any of the times professional wrestling legend Randy "Macho Man" Savage was a guest on *The Arsenio Hall Show*, which reminded you of once telling a partner, "But Jake 'the Snake' and the Undertaker ruined 'Macho Man' and Elizabeth's wedding," like it was a perfectly reasonable excuse to not get married.

— 21 —

Today you remembered that dating is just a means in finding someone who will temporarily cure your internet porn addiction.

— 22 —

Today you tried changing your Facebook relationship status to "It's Complicated," but it was too complicated.

— 23 —

Today you wondered if you were the only sad person in this world who thinks Marvin Gaye's 1982 hit "Sexual Healing" is the least sexy song of all time.

— 24 —

Today you dwelled on a random past regret.

— 25 —

Today you spoke to someone on the phone while they were gagging and coughing and complaining about having to smoke weed laced with their dog's hair because they'd rolled a joint with it resting on their couch instead of a nearby table, which is a nice reminder of the kinds of people you choose to love in this life.

— 26 —

Today you compulsively took someone's offhand remark that probably meant nothing and turned it into *Gone with the Wind 2*.

— 27 —

Today your love came wrapped inside of a grease-soaked paper bag.

— 28 —

Today you imagined being in a relationship where feeding your partner Arby's curly fries while watching *Gilmore Girls* was as intimate as it ever got.

— 29 —

Today you tenderly asked the half-eaten, dust-covered McDonald's Chicken McNugget found on your bedroom floor to marry you.

MARCH

— 1 —

Today you'd spiritually identified as one of those commercials about depression where a person is just staring morosely out of a window.

Today you befuddled someone by randomly saying, "Let's not beat around the Kate Bush, all right?"

— 3 —

Today you tried making a statement by playing your emotions like pieces in a chess game but being that you don't even know how to properly play checkers made it a weak statement.

— 4 —

Today you gradually came to grips with the sad fact that the only thing you and your stepdad ever had in common was a mutual appreciation for the comedic stylings of Jeff Foxworthy.

—5—

Today you considered petitioning Comedy Central to bring back that useless trivia show *Beat the Geeks*, because only then would your limited potential be fully realized.

—6—

Today you had a very confusing wet dream about living in a tool shed where there were no tools and it was just you but, like, it was still called a tool shed.

—7—

Today, after a co-worker asked if you'd caught the latest episode of *Stranger Things*, you shook your head and told them your favorite TV show was actually *Saved by the Bell* and that you should automatically get hired as a high school principal because of all the episodes you've seen, but they weren't impressed.

—8—

Today you became surprisingly jealous of a TV show that got cancelled because you'd like to be cancelled too.

—9—

Today you told a group of hipsters that *Full House* was your favorite Iggy and the Stooges record.

—10—

Today you studiously watched YouTube tutorials on how to make homemade versions of those Teenage Mutant Ninja Turtles vanilla pudding pies that were inexplicably discontinued in the '90s.

Today you wondered if anyone has ever named their kid(s) Bebop (and) or Rocksteady, and whether or not that is even legal.

Today you considered making a shitty hand puppet à la Triumph the Insult Comic Dog but calling it "Failure the Insult Comic Frog," then harassing strangers on the street with it.

Today you were evicted from all twelve zodiac houses.

— 14 —

Today you pretended that your phone was a Tamagotchi pet screaming to be fed validation.

— 15 —

Today you complimented someone's healthy upbringing by offering them a fist bump and saying, "No broken home-o!"

— 16 —

Today you remembered that you're more of a no-never than a go-getter.

— 17 —

Today you tried convincing people that St. Patrick's Day was now called Dollar Tree Employee Appreciation Day, which resulted in slight disappointment.

— 18 —

Today you told someone, "Oh man, this is awesome," while thinking, *I'm freaking the fuck out!*

— 19 —

Today you communicated solely via downloaded ALF JPEGs you hoard in a desktop folder labeled "I Kill Me."

— 20 —

Today you watched medical-themed porn because you don't have health insurance and can't afford to go to a real doctor.

— 21 —

Today you sexually identified as an empty vessel.

— 22 —

Today you found yourself in that kooky place where being a cartoon version of a depressed person and an actual depressed person meet.

Today, after being threatened with violence, you nervously listed off the many professional wrestling holds you thought you knew, starting with "arm bar."

Today you fantasized about slamming professional wrestling star John Cena through a flaming table that was covered in thumbtacks, freshly dug-up *E.T.* Atari video game cartridges, and broken copies of all four KISS solo LPs.

Today you sexually identified as a rock bottom.

— 26 —

Today you browsed the Walmart frozen desserts section with both confusion and gravitas, like it was a fine art exhibit.

— 27 —

Today you watched a YouTube video showing you how to properly pronounce words like "gravitas."

— 28 —

Today your life felt like a dumb, inappropriate dad joke and only you were laughing.

— 29 —

Today you experienced a moment of Zen while watching a woman at the deli squeeze macaroni and cheese out of a plastic bag.

— 30 —

Today you pecked away at your *John Wick* screenplay, the one where Keanu Reeves is now a server at The Cheesecake Factory and he must hunt down and kill an entire party he waited on because they didn't leave him a slice of birthday cake as gratuity.

— 31 —

Today you considered going on an Easter egg hunt for dopamine and serotonin.

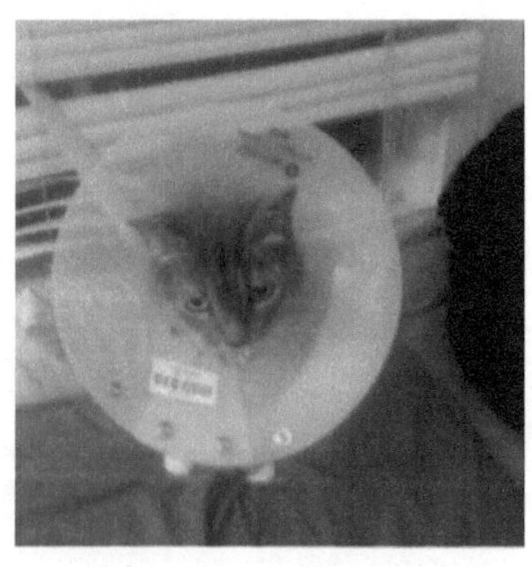

APRIL

— 1 —

Today you built resentment as though it were the LEGO of your adulthood.

— 2 —

Today you walked out into the rainy shit weather and very aggressively said to it, "Oh, you think you fucking know me, son?"

— 3 —

Today you had a super uplifting wet dream where you were a princess in some *Sims-/Animal Crossing*-like video game who ran around different villages, collecting treasures and killing Nazis.

— 4 —

Today you hesitated when putting a dirty knife into a sink full of dirty dishes because you feared you'd never see it again.

— 5 —

Today, after having only gone to the post office, you marked yourself as "safe" on Facebook.

— 6 —

Today you tried figuring out ways to amuse yourself without drinking too much and freaking out the people around you/yourself.

— 7 —

Today you imagined dropping heroic acid doses at Dollywood, which would then turn it into Daliwood.

Today you wondered how much more insufferable you could possibly get before your drug dealers finally cut you off.

Today you sighed heavily before turning to your cat and saying, "So, seriously, what are we doing with our lives?"

Today you subsisted on kindness.

Today you subsisted on the broken remnants at the bottom of an Extreme Queso Grande Doritos bag.

Today, while in the mood for some real shenanigans, you got high off bleach fumes in a dark, warm, poorly ventilated room with your cat.

Today you listened to Rancid while reminiscing about the dog collars you'd steal from PetSmart, which you wore during your high school ska-punk phase.

— 14 —

Today you listened to even more Rancid (and maybe also the Mighty Mighty Bosstones) while reminiscing about drawing 2-Tone checkers on the straps of your JanSport backpack using Wite-Out Correction Fluid, which also occurred during your high school ska-punk phase.

— 15 —

Today you were gripped by the sudden fear of having once gone through a rockabilly phase without even realizing it.

— 16 —

Today, to see what you'll probably look like in the very near future, you image-googled "old fat rockabilly," which resulted in slight disappointment.

— 17 —

Today you noticed that everyone you know over thirty is starting to look and act really weird.

— 18 —

Today you randomly yelled and made odd grunting noises to remind yourself, and your cat, that *Hey, I'm still alive!*

— 19 —

Today, while reheating only a sips-worth of coffee in hopes of temporarily repairing your damaged psyche, you realized that the best part of waking up would be to not wake up.

— 20 —

Today you rolled and then smoked a fat bout of crippling depression.

— 21 —

Today you randomly ended a conversation by saying, "Aerosmith—three weeks," before casually walking away.

— 22 —

Today you couldn't stop thinking about that couple you saw on *Hoarders* who had a bowl full of defective vibrators they hoped to one day use for an art project.

—23—

Today you fantasized about one day hosting a show called *Unsolved Miseries*, where you'd creepily stalk a 7-Eleven parking lot at night while wearing a trench coat and drinking a Slurpee.

—24—

Today you composed an elaborate e-mail that was basically just an apology to someone for being a stupid dumpster human.

—25—

Today you attempted to build back trust from someone you don't trust while also exploring new and exciting ways of not trusting yourself.

— 26 —

Today you typed "LOL" while actually feeling nothing inside.

— 27 —

Today you spiritually identified as the Pigeon Lady from *Home Alone 2: Lost in New York* (1992).

— 28 —

Today you issued an open invitation for people to move on from whatever it is you are.

— 29 —

Today, while overhearing someone say to another person over the phone, "It was an accident," you automatically assumed that you were the accident they were referring to.

— 30 —

Today you imagined yourself shouting, "Whoopsie, gotta go, found my tribe!" before jumping into a pile of burning garbage, never to be seen or heard from again.

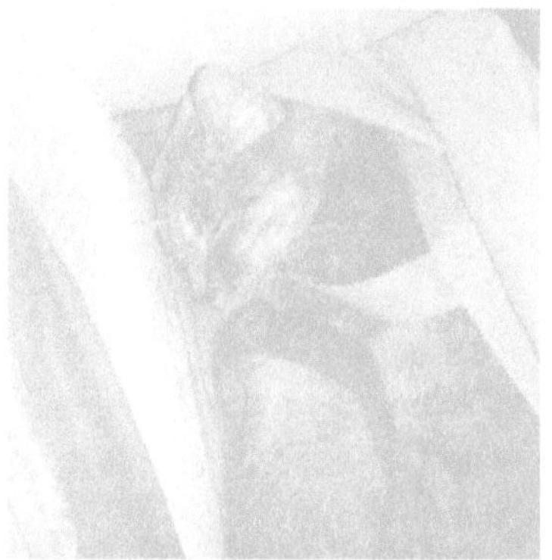

MAY

— 1 —

Today you told a visitor to "excuse the mess," referring to not only your cluttered apartment but also the unseen mess that exists within yourself.

— 2 —

Today you spiritually identified as the soul of a sixty-year-old cat lady with hoarding tendencies.

— 3 —

Today, hoping to find assistance with your debilitating self-loathing, you contacted the Twitter Help Center.

— 4 —

Today, as a form of self-torture, you put yourself in an awkward situation.

— 5 —

Today, instead of Mexican food, you tried making a statement by only eating fried bologna sandwiches on Cinco de Mayo, though fried bologna sandwiches are pretty much what you eat every day, which made it a weak statement.

— 6 —

Today you imagined having a "yard sale" where you just lie on the couch in your pajamas while looking at Facebook as random people come into your apartment to take whatever they want, maybe utilizing the haphazardly placed tip jar on their way out.

— 7 —

Today you renamed your cat ROCKY IV.

— 8 —

Today, after being snapped out of a daze, you said to someone, "Oh sorry, was just plotting my revenge."

— 9 —

Today you pictured yourself exploding into something called "disappointment confetti," and smiled.

— 10 —

Today you fantasized about spending a weekend watching cable TV in someone's guest bedroom, alone.

— 11 —

Today you thought about one day moving into someone's garage but not the whole garage, mind you; just a small section of the garage where you wouldn't be in the way of the person's Prius or anything.

— 12 —

Today you tried making a statement by celebrating Mother's Day at the mall food court, which (as usual) resulted in yet another weak statement.

— 13 —

Today you thought about all those times you had to move back in with your mom and how she always feared that one day it would be permanent, but nothing is permanent, which is exactly why you'd have to keep moving back in with her.

— 14 —

Today you imagined a *Back to the Future* reboot where, after returning to the year you were born, you try convincing your mom to have an abortion.

— 15 —

Today you fantasized about one day winning a *Back to the Future 2*-replica Hoverboard on eBay while having a midlife crisis and then sticking it in a corner somewhere forever.

— 16 —

Today you found it incredibly difficult to live in a world where, according to some Reddit article, Trent Reznor doesn't "get" Drake.

— 17 —

Today you watched a YouTube video of Nine Inch Nails performing at Woodstock '94, which reminded you of middle school and how miserable you were that summer, which involved being terrorized by a kid in your trailer park and having to hide indoors watching the OJ Simpson trial with your mom, though you may just be subconsciously combining two miserable summers.

— 18 —

Today you reminded someone that, when it comes to friendship, your biggest attribute is how you metaphorically make for a nice, empty garbage bin people can scream into.

— 19 —

Today you felt personally attacked when someone sent you a blue thumbs up on Facebook messenger.

— 20 —

Today you updated your resume while eating a fried bologna sandwich and thinking about death.

— 21 —

Today you realized that handing someone a resume is
like handing them future garbage that cost about fifteen
cents to produce.

— 22 —

Today you started filling out applications for the dream
job of actually liking yourself before quickly noticing how
short on references you were.

Today you scammed a ride to Walmart to purchase cat food and knock-off brand breakfast cereal before ditching the person you were with to go eat at the Walmart McDonald's by yourself.

Today you wondered if the person who created the McDonald's Hamburglar is real proud of themselves.

Today you stared into the abyss, and as the abyss stared back you immediately thought of how weird you must've looked because of your body dysmorphia.

— 26 —

Today, when not enough people acknowledged your clever social media post, you checked your pulse for some kind of life worth living.

— 27 —

Today, while going down a YouTube rabbit hole of '90s songs, you spiritually identified as that one Third Eye Blind music video where the guy may or may not leap from a large building.

— 28 —

Today, while listening listlessly to podcasts about serial killers and eating fried bologna sandwiches, you'd occasionally scold your cat for continuing to scratch up an already scratched-up couch.

— 29 —

Today you remained the strangest roommate you've ever had.

— 30 —

Today you had a very stressful wet dream about attending a disastrous Taylor Swift concert held in the parking lot behind a deli where a kid who tried running up on stage got caught and then popped in the face really hard by his dad, which means your slowly deteriorating mental health says, "Sup?"

— 31 —

Today you imagined Death coming to pick you up in an Uber, and you both casually being like, "Oh hey," as you got in.

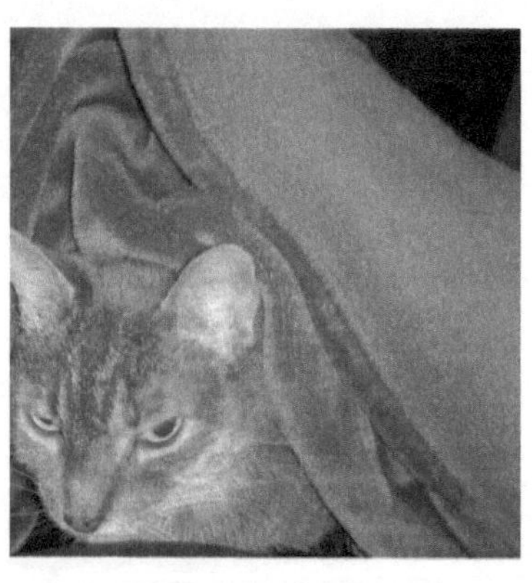

JUNE

— 1 —

Today you realized that the only reason you drink and do drugs is to stand your own company.

— 2 —

Today you canceled plans based on the "unreasonable" fear that your cat would most likely be set on fire if you left the apartment.

— 3 —

Today you continued to think negatively about things as though it were some superstitious habit.

— 4 —

Today you depressed a co-worker in their twenties by embodying what they'll probably have to look forward to in their thirties.

—5—

Today you were saddened to report that the poster in your middle school health class depicting members of '80s pop group Cameo karate chopping a ridiculously large cigarette with the slogan "Break It, Don't Take It!" did not keep you from smoking or using copious amounts of drugs.

—6—

Today you watched a neighbor swap what appeared to be two identically ugly sofa chairs in and out of their apartment as the *Dog the Bounty Hunter* theme song blared in the background.

—7—

Today you karate chopped a semi-broken lamp.

$$- 8 -$$

Today you head-butted a paper towel dispenser.

$$- 9 -$$

Today you thought about randomly turning to your co-workers and shouting, "YOU'RE ALL GONNA DIE HERE!" before adding in a wicked cackle or something.

$$- 10 -$$

Today you rated and reviewed all the recent panic attacks you've had at work via random household items sold on Amazon dot com.

—11—

Today you felt sophisticated as your usual fits of psychic terror were occasionally tempered by general malaise.

—12—

Today your personal growth was diagnosed "malignant."

—13—

Today, while in the mood for some real shenanigans, you considered investing in an ice cream truck business where you ride around blasting R.E.M's 1993 hit "Everybody Hurts" as the inventory melts.

— 14 —

Today you considered opening an Etsy store that only sells XXL hoodies with a picture printed on the back of just your screaming face.

— 15 —

Today you irrationally linked the start of your emotional unraveling to the exact moment Cher's "Believe" hit #1 on Billboard's Hot 100.

— 16 —

Today you misread someone's "Happy Father's Day to all the men in my life who are dads" Facebook post as "Happy Father's Day to all the men in my life who are dead," which resulted in slight disappointment.

— 17 —

Today, while singing along to Madonna's 1989 hit "Express Yourself" at a bar, you cleverly changed the word "express" to "depress," but nobody seemed impressed.

— 18 —

Today, instead of a resume, you considered bringing the first three Danzig albums to a job interview and then just taking it from there.

— 19 —

Today you purchased a belt from Family Dollar.

— 20 —

Today your self-worth took too long to load.

— 21 —

Today you considered live-tweeting a YouTube viewing of someone's VHS rip of the 1991 MTV Video Music Awards, asking if people thought society was statistically more motivated when listening to the music of C+C Music Factory or whatever.

— 22 —

Today you posted multiple Instagram photos of your cat sleeping inside of a Domino's box, thus renaming her PIZZA POINTS.

Today, after asking hipsters at some party if they were "feelin' some 'Smooth Criminal'," you put on the Alien Ant Farm version.

Today, after asking your cat if she was "ready to fuck shit up," you put on the remastered version of *Tea for the Tillerman* by Cat Stevens.

Today you considered hiring Dr. Dre (or maybe Rick Rubin) to produce your serotonin.

Today you reminisced about the days when JUUL was a yodeling Canadian singer-songstress moonlighting as a best-selling poet who supposedly lived out of a car, and not just some vaping apparatus one randomly finds on the dirty floors of bars and/or tucked between Uber seat cushions late at night.

Today you befuddled someone by randomly saying, "Imagine infiltrating some nondescript inner circle while listening to the *Cops* theme by Inner Circle."

Today you told someone, "Hey, look on the bright side," while thinking: *Darkness / Imprisoning me / All that I see / Absolute horror!*

Today, to cope with ongoing stepdad trauma, you listened to a '90s country playlist on Spotify.

Today, while binge-watching random YouTube videos of Beavis and Butthead binge-watching random music videos, you may have asked yourself, "Well, how did I get here?"

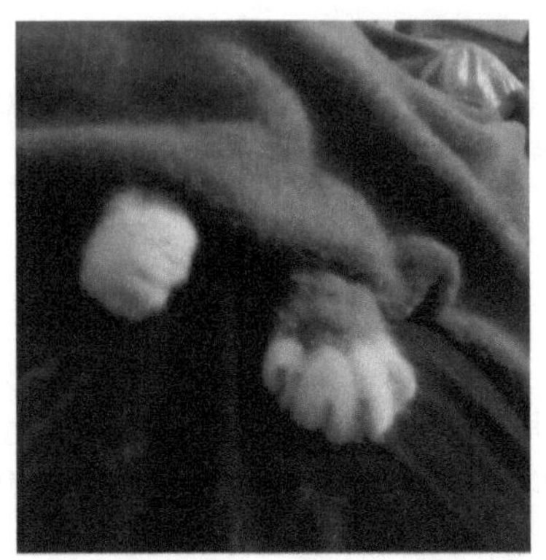

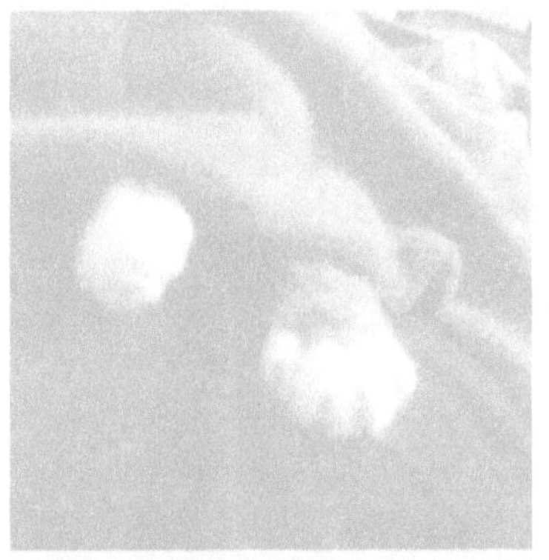

JULY

— 1 —

Today you gave your inability to deal with anything a negative review on Yelp dot com.

— 2 —

Today, as you exited the room your cat was in, you asked whether she wanted the light on or off.

— 3 —

Today you waited for the stoned Jamaican delivery driver to call saying he was lost, even though he gets lost bringing Chinese food to your apartment more often than you'd care to admit.

— 4 —

Today, while people either swam or grilled hot dogs and burgers, you sat in a shaded patio chair for hours, pounding warm cans of Pabst Blue Ribbon, smoking cigarettes, downing Jell-O shots, and thinking about death.

— 5 —

Today you bragged to hipsters at some party about only doing keg stands ironically.

— 6 —

Today you resumed your ongoing performance art piece where you pretend to like and/or respect the person you're interacting with at any given moment, especially while at work.

— 7 —

Today you counted the number of times a co-worker used the hashtag "BROstaRica" when posting Instagram photos of his Costa Rica trip.

$$- 8 -$$

Today you kept tabs on the many co-workers you'd like to one day roundhouse kick in the face à la Chuck Norris.

$$- 9 -$$

Today you pecked away at your *Look Who's Talking Meow* screenplay, the one where your cat has the uncanny ability to roundhouse kick your co-workers in the face à la Chuck Norris.

$$- 10 -$$

Today you filled the vast emptiness inside yourself with handfuls of peanut M&Ms.

Today, with the same languid despair of Harry Dean Stanton's character in *Paris, Texas* (1984), you roamed aimlessly around town in search of an Applebee's.

Today you pictured yourself floating through life like that plastic bag in *American Beauty* (1999) but, like, maybe the bag is tied up because there's dog shit inside of it or whatever.

Today you thought about reenacting the scene from *Heathers* (1988) where the overweight girl wearing the "Big Fun" t-shirt purposely walks into oncoming traffic, though you'd instead be wearing a t-shirt that has "The Dream Died" (or "Dream's Dead") (or "Dreams R.I.P.") printed on it.

— 14 —

Today, like a real Rockefeller, you walked to the corner store for cat food, one roll of toilet paper, one bar of soap, a bag of Spicy Nacho Doritos, and an apple-flavored Hostess pastry.

— 15 —

Today, as a treat, you let your cat lick the mental illness from your armpit hair.

— 16 —

Today you resumed your ongoing performance art piece where you watch shitty movies while eating shitty food and resent anything that gets in the way of that.

— 17 —

Today you had one of those reoccurring nightmares where you're either getting left back in high school, uselessly wandering the aisles of an empty Forever 21, or just watching TV with your stepdad.

— 18 —

Today you compulsively repeated the phrase "nightmare person" while self-reflecting in the shower.

— 19 —

Today you gauged the level of your own full-of-shittedness by the number of times you used the word "absolutely" in conversation.

— 20 —

Today you remembered that one of your only joys in life consists of eavesdropping on co-workers as they explain, in detail, how they foolishly blew their entire paychecks in one night, which means that life's simple pleasures are still basically awful.

— 21 —

Today you spiritually identified as an optical illusion painting where, when you look closely enough, a capsized sailboat pops out.

— 22 —

Today you resumed your ongoing performance art piece where you smoke cigarettes while waiting around for dumb shit to happen.

— 23 —

Today you were told that you basically live like a crack-
head who doesn't smoke crack.

— 24 —

Today you found the loneliest bar in town—one that
smelled like piss, vomit and cigarettes, and where someone was performing karaoke to Madonna's 1989 hit "Like
a Prayer"—and just, like, sat there for what seemed like a
long, long time.

— 25 —

Today you absentmindedly tripped over a large dog re-
sembling a wolf that either Danzig or Jack London would
probably own.

Today you had a frustrating wet dream where you got mad at Google+ for letting everyone know that you watched a Spin Doctors video on Vimeo, like it's anyone's damn business.

Today you considered petitioning for a law to be passed where extroverts are required to Venmo introverts before engaging them in any unwarranted conversation.

Today you saw the best minds of your generation destroyed by drunk texts.

— 29 —

Today, while singing along to Bachman-Turner Over-
drive's 1973 hit "Takin' Care of Business" at a bar, you
cleverly changed the word "business" to "abyssness," but
nobody seemed impressed.

— 30 —

Today you metaphorically picked the wrong people to be
on your kickball team.

— 31 —

Today you continued going through the motions of being
a human being and found no real joy or purpose in it, but
whatever.

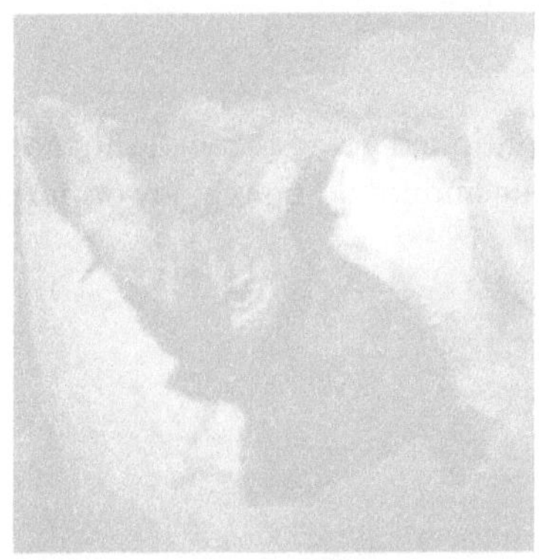

AUGUST

— 1 —

Today you got annoyed at your one personality for getting your other personalities into the current mess they're in.

— 2 —

Today you recycled all your junk mail into a found art project entitled "Miranda July Swag."

— 3 —

Today you convinced yourself that the internet is now your "forever home."

— 4 —

Today you were insulted when a co-worker told you, "You won't be disappointed," because that's like someone calling your initial reaction towards everything a lie, which is rude.

— 5 —

Today, to seem cool, you lied when telling someone that the "Teenage Mutant Ninja Turtles: Coming out of Their Shells Tour" was your first concert experience, which is all anyone really needs to know about you as a person.

— 6 —

Today, after finding someone's receipt inside of a book checked out from the library, you casually stalked the person online because, regardless of whether the book is any good or not, you still kind of want their opinion on it.

— 7 —

Today you considered launching a Kickstarter campaign to help fund a product called Struggie™, which (unlike a Snuggie®) is basically a torn blanket from childhood that struggling, depressed adults can cry into.

Today, while in the mood for some real shenanigans, you intensely browsed the Starbucks CD rack of Michael Bublé-endorsed jazz standards like someone searching for the collectible first pressing of some rare LP.

Today you muttered to co-workers, "Wow, what a come-apart," before having to face yet another shift of more come-apart action.

Today, when asked how you've been, you sighed heavily and said, "Another day, another dollar-brand mac and cheese dinner eaten straight from the pot," then winked.

— 11 —

Today you considered making a (weak?) statement by getting "Mac N' Cheese" tattooed in Old English lettering on your lower back with the Great Value™ logo inked directly above it.

— 12 —

Today you compulsively picked at emotional wounds like they were tattoos that never heal.

— 13 —

Today you remembered that you have absolutely no business doing anything which requires more effort than just napping and visiting random buffets.

— 14 —

Today you turned to your cat and said, in a highly questionable Italian chef voice, "You wanna more water? I give you more water. You wanna more love? I give you more love."

— 15 —

Today you had an existential crisis to Sir Mix-a-Lot's "Baby Got Back" while at a '90s-themed dance night.

— 16 —

Today you did not claim your Domino's "pizza points," mainly because you feel that self-destructive behavior shouldn't always be rewarded.

— 17 —

Today you had an especially emotional wet dream where, on an episode of *Shark Tank*, you tried convincing Mark Cuban to help save your failing *My Little Pony*-themed pizza parlor (Brony's Calzoneys).

— 18 —

Today you asked someone why food porn wasn't just called "feastiality," but they didn't know.

— 19 —

Today you spiritually identified as a sideways baseball cap with "wasted my thirties being sad on the internet" printed on it.

— 20 —

Today you imagined hosting a successful game show called *So You Think You Can Block Toxic Behavioral Patterns?*

— 21 —

Today you considered jumping out of a moving vehicle, though you weren't even inside a moving vehicle at the time.

— 22 —

Today you sexually identified as a busted rear-view mirror hanging off a car that the owner is too lazy and/or broke to fix.

— 23 —

Today you were triggered by "safety features."

— 24 —

Today you frantically searched for your car keys before realizing that you don't even own a car.

— 25 —

Today, in conversation, you somehow confused a chapter from *Don Quixote* with an episode of *Walker Texas Ranger*.

— 26 —

Today you randomly befuddled someone by dubbing yourself the Windows 95 of useless trivia knowledge.

— 27 —

Today you could've *easily* depression-eaten an entire birthday cake.

— 28 —

Today you renamed your cat COBRA KAI: SEASON 2 FINALE.

– 29 –

Today you went up to a new co-worker who was just standing around and said, "If you got time to lean, you got time to let your thoughts bravely navigate the shame and despair which constitutes the existential vacuum within," but they weren't impressed.

– 30 –

Today you realized that you've been alive for too long.

– 31 –

Today, when stopping to admire a dead squirrel on the sidewalk, you urgently whispered to yourself, "Soon," and continued walking.

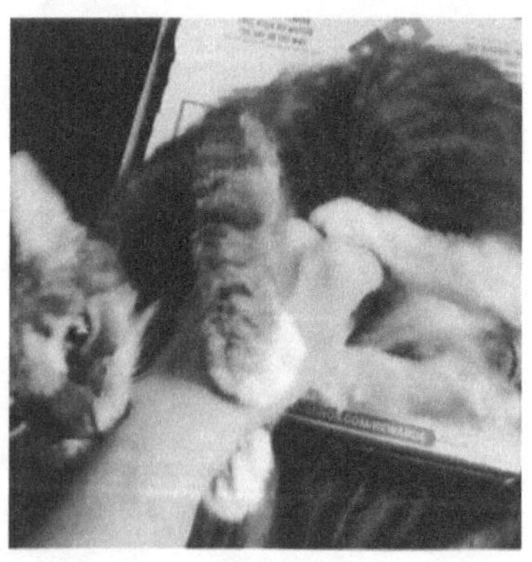

SEPTEMBER

— 1 —

Today you continued letting your life fall apart with the same indifference as watching a shitty reality show about someone else's life falling apart.

$$-2-$$

Today you once again suppressed the sleepy, just-to-see-what'll-happen urge to pee on your cat when she came into the bathroom at 7 a.m. wanting to be fed.

$$-3-$$

Today you told someone, "We make a killer team," while thinking, *Oh God don't look at me!*

$$-4-$$

Today you considered celebrating your birthday by getting drunk off peppermint schnapps and then beating someone mercilessly with cat furniture before jumping through a window.

Today you sexually identified as the soul of a dead clown.

Today you fantasized about having a car, but just so you could tell passengers that the miniature garbage can hanging from the rear-view mirror was actually your "dream catcher."

Today you wondered whether tollbooth operators could provide drivers with spiritual change.

— 8 —

Today you told someone that you could burn calories faster by forgetting to eat because of depression, but they weren't impressed.

— 9 —

Today you imagined getting paid big bucks to "flat tire" the backs of people's shoes as you strode behind them with their wealthy, giggling enemies.

— 10 —

Today you renamed your cat DEGRASSI.

— 11 —

Today you judged the names of other people's pets that were written on the dry erase board at the vet clinic.

— 12 —

Today you considered treating certain people as though they were really cute dogs, grabbing them behind the ears and cooing, "Aww, who's a seemingly well-adjusted person capable of living in the moment, is it you?? Yes you are, YES YOU ARE!!"

— 13 —

Today you refused to be publicly shamed by the monsters you work with who think it's peculiar that you consistently walk around covered in your cat's hair.

— 14 —

Today you were triggered by someone who said they wanted a baby.

— 15 —

Today you were triggered by someone who said they had a baby.

— 16 —

Today you shouted, "Alexa, was the Sermon on the Mount featuring Jesus the first act to headline Coachella?" but Alexa didn't know.

— 17 —

Today you considered making hemp-style necklaces out of cat shedding to maybe wear and/or sell via a vending tent at Burning Man.

— 18 —

Today you used fun phrases like "I Can't Even Stevens starring Shia LaBeouf!" while feeling crushed by the weight of the world.

— 19 —

Today you thought about dying, and instead of your life, having every Nicolas Cage meme ever created flash before your eyes.

— 20 —

Today you muted random people on Twitter to make room for more tweets by bootleg rappers.

— 21 —

Today you cheekily told a co-worker that you were up for the job of fixing the internet every time someone says something has broken it, and they said, "Like an IT person?" and you said, "What? No. Never mind," and walked away dejected, but only momentarily.

— 22 —

Today, while attempting to remove toxic people from your life, you remembered that the most toxic person you know is still you.

— 23 —

Today you apologized to the people you drank heavily with the night before by saying, "Sorry I made you listen to all that emo."

— 24 —

Today you were gripped by the sudden fear that the music video for Yellowcard's 2003 hit "Ocean Avenue" might be one of the tabs left open on your laptop once your rotting, half-eaten corpse is discovered amongst a bunch of indifferent trash animals.

— 25 —

Today you tried finding an outlet that doesn't involve screaming into pillows in a sun-deprived bedroom as your frightened cat looks on.

— 26 —

Today you told someone that you could burn calories faster by aimlessly walking around because of anxiety, but they weren't impressed.

— 27 —

Today you nurtured the ongoing ache of wanting to contact people you think are mad at you but at the same time scared they might actually forgive you and, like, want to "hang out sometime."

— 28 —

Today you successfully evaded the co-worker who once insisted, "If I can do it, anyone can."

— 29 —

Today you fancied yourself as someone smart enough to engineer a strap-on bomb that could only detonate when giving someone a fist bump.

— 30 —

Today you threatened to sue yourself for emotional damages.

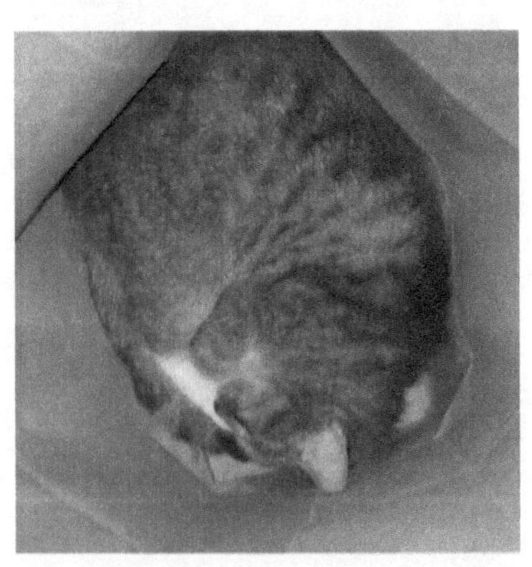

OCTOBER

— 1 —

Today you wore black on the outside because black is how you felt on the ~~inside~~ internet.

— 2 —

Today you remained haunted by everything.

— 3 —

Today you told someone about how you're not so much into True Crime as you are into true crying.

— 4 —

Today you called bullshit on those scary movie trailers on TV where they show night vision footage of audience members jumping out of their seats and screaming but zero footage of people playing with their cell phones or sleeping or masturbating.

— 5 —

Today you considered turning all your bad decisions into a commercially successful horror movie franchise.

— 6 —

Today you resisted the nagging, just-to-see-what'll-happen urge to put on a Ghostface mask from *Scream* (1996) and shout, "Waaahhhzzzuuup!?" into a random person's face.

— 7 —

Today you pecked away at your *Boohoobusters* screenplay, the one where a ragtag team of pro ass-kissers comment on whiny Facebook meltdown posts with vapid, pseudo-motivational clichés.

— 8 —

Today you hexed whoever borrowed but then didn't return your DVD with all the *Roseanne* Halloween episodes on it.

— 9 —

Today you spiritually identified as a demonic hellhole that spews evil after someone throws a dead dog in it.

— 10 —

Today you decided to ask anyone you ever meet whether they've been to a monster truck rally and then just taking it from there.

— 11 —

Today you thought about attending a Halloween party dressed as "Multiple Personality Disorder Visibly Uncomfortable Being Around Other Personality Disorders," then allowing all of your personalities to lap around the party before having them meet up with you later.

— 12 —

Today you felt suffocated by your reality, like it was a haunted Halloween mask you couldn't remove.

— 13 —

Today you spiritually identified as the old drunk in every horror movie who warns the horny teenagers about all the scary shit that's about to go down.

— 14 —

Today you renamed your cat RUNTIE JAMES DIO.

— 15 —

Today you got lost in the spooky corn maze of your mind.

— 16 —

Today you treated your body like it was either Nickelodeon's *Legends of the Hidden Temple* (only after the show was canceled and all the sets were gutted) or 1984's *Indiana Jones and the Temple of Doom* (where random people either fall off shitty rope bridges or they have their hearts ripped from their chest).

— 17 —

Today you tried getting your ~~life~~ death together.

— 18 —

Today you jumped from one worst-case scenario to the next, which was admittedly the most exercise you'd gotten in a while.

— 19 —

Today you told someone that you had officially sold the exclusive streaming rights to all your current and future emotional breakdowns to the internet, but they weren't impressed.

Today you considered introducing yourself to the new co-worker by telling them, "Hey, I dig both thrash-metal Death and proto-punk Death, and also, like, *Faces of Death* and *Death of a Salesman*, and actual death, so we fuckin' gonna party, or what!?"

Today you were triggered by a "dumpster match" they had on an episode of *Monday Night Raw*.

Today you tried convincing your mom to go as professional wrestling legend Mankind for Halloween.

— 23 —

Today you were uncharacteristically proud of yourself for correctly typing out the name "Schwarzenegger" without cheating.

— 24 —

Today you were frightened of young people, and old people, and people roughly your own age, and people exactly your own age.

— 25 —

Today, gripping your pillows tight, you listened as your new upstairs neighbor, a DJ, tried making an EDM remix of Metallica's 1991 hit "Enter Sandman."

— 26 —

Today you had to say to your cat, "Don't judge," as she stared hard at a man zooming by in a motorized wheel-chair with his dog trailing behind on a leash.

— 27 —

Today you tried kicking in a door while listening to 1995's *Jagged Little Pill*, the Grammy-winning album from Canadian songstress Alanis Morissette.

— 28 —

Today you made things worse.

— 29 —

Today, while broodily drinking a Pabst Blue Ribbon in the alleyway outside of a bar with the 1994 Nine Inch Nails hit "Hurt" blaring from your phone, concerned strangers walked by asking, "You good?"

— 30 —

Today you remembered that sometimes the only way to cope in a world of such terror is to drink and do drugs on a stranger's back patio at 6 a.m. while someone drops a needle on the LP version of *The Lost Boys: Original Motion Picture Soundtrack*.

— 31 —

Today, after putting a white plastic bag over your head, you tried convincing co-workers that a "Sexy Cloud of E-Cig Vapor" Halloween costume was a good idea.

NOVEMBER

— 1 —

Today you sexually identified as a dead mall.

— 2 —

Today you had a super realistic wet dream where you went around asking people why they hate you.

— 3 —

Today you randomly befuddled someone by saying, "How are we expected to save daylight when we can't even save ourselves?"

— 4 —

Today you wondered why people still care about sports, or anything.

– 5 –

Today you tried living your best ~~life~~ escape from reality.

– 6 –

Today you considered murdering your upstairs neighbor for loudly singing along to an EDM remix of Neil Diamond's 1969 hit "Sweet Caroline," and for being young, happy and carefree, and for being a DJ.

– 7 –

Today you imagined yourself as a lazy stripper who performs "nap" dances instead of "lap" dances, which are the only dances that matter besides "dirty" and ones involving wolves.

— 8 —

Today you continued to suppress the nagging urge to just
run away and go die somewhere alone.

— 9 —

Today you had an inspiring wet dream where you were in
a super violent professional wrestling match and you
were calling spots and going through tables and it was
the happiest, most accomplished you've ever felt—and
you didn't even win!—and when you woke up, you noticed your pillow was slobbered on because you were
spitting blood in the dream.

— 10 —

Today you reluctantly tried forcing yourself outside of a
comfort zone that doesn't even really exist.

Today you automatically disliked something that someone thought you'd really like.

Today you reviewed a magazine's masthead while urgently whispering to yourself, "Must identify the leader of this operation and take them down."

Today you fantasized about one day being featured in a prestigious magazine like *Rolling Stone*, but only as the person wearing a bootleg Sublime shirt in one of those ads in the very back.

— 14 —

Today you ignored the many life mistakes you've made by obsessing over the tiny editorial mistakes you've made.

— 15 —

Today you told someone, "Things are really starting to happen for us," while thinking, *I've never felt more alone.*

— 16 —

Today you realized that to escape depression, you habitually put yourself in depressing situations.

— 17 —

Today you spiritually identified as that nutty neighbor who hoards animals, sits alone in their car to listen to public radio, and often urinates drunkenly on their own stoop.

— 18 —

Today you had a bittersweet wet dream where your ex finally acknowledged the texts you'd sent them.

— 19 —

Today you kept being one of those zany people who must have every single positive feeling murdered inside of them before they finally get the hint.

Today you didn't catch a lot of breaks, though you did catch many brokens.

Today you practiced retail therapy by purchasing enough drugs and alcohol to momentarily numb the pain of living.

Today you resumed your ongoing performance art piece where you hit the town and get fucked up while feeling super uncomfortable about everything.

— 23 —

Today you ruined something that wasn't worth it over something that also wasn't worth it.

— 24 —

Today you purchased expensive skincare products online for your highly ungrateful cat.

— 25 —

Today you tried tying Twizzlers into a noose you'd hoped to maybe hang yourself with.

— 26 —

Today you packed for a trip, which means you just threw a bunch of semi-dirty t-shirts and underwear into a scented GLAD trash bag while trying not to spill your Diet Dr Pepper.

— 27 —

Today you remembered that the best part about flying is when the flight attendant goes up and down the aisle asking for trash, because that's your time to really shine.

— 28 —

Today you associated Thanksgiving with Neil Young's coke booger from *The Last Waltz* (1978).

— 29 —

Today you resumed your ongoing performance art piece
of frying bologna while low-key waiting for death to happen.

— 30 —

Today you didn't learn your lesson.

DECEMBER

— 1 —

Today you tested negative for positivity.

— 2 —

Today you were curiously alarmed by the number of David Arquette movies you own on VHS.

— 3 —

Today, instead of putting up a Christmas tree, you put up more emotional walls to better dissociate from people this holiday season, thus finally earning your dissociates degree.

— 4 —

Today you remembered that longing and dread are both Christmas movies.

$$-5-$$

Today you wondered if you were the only sad person in this world intrigued that so many Merle Haggard Christmas albums exist.

$$-6-$$

Today you considered ordering a Guy Fieri cookbook online to maybe give to someone's mom on Christmas.

$$-7-$$

Today you intensely stared into the bathroom mirror while muttering to yourself, "Ernest went to camp, saved Christmas, went to jail, got scared stupid and then was a basketball player or something—the fuck have *you* done?" before spitting at your reflection.

— 8 —

Today you pecked away at your *Scrooged 2* screenplay, the one where David Johansen reprises his role as the cigar-chewing cabbie who, after being visited by the ghosts of all the dead members of the New York Dolls, repeatedly runs you over with his cab.

— 9 —

Today you enjoyed seeing the sudden spiritual erosion and grievous heartbreak happening on someone's face after they were told, "No, sorry, we don't have ranch dressing."

— 10 —

Today you attempted to "live in the moment" by sharing ice cream with your cat.

— 11 —

Today you told someone, "Yeah, yeah, let's meet up," while thinking: *The world is a vampire...*

— 12 —

Today you had a tasty wet dream where professional wrestling star John Cena shoved you inside of a denim-covered coffin, which was bedazzled with thumbtacks and then set on fire as the 1992 Guns N' Roses hit "November Rain" blared in the background.

— 13 —

Today you had an even tastier wet dream where professional wrestling star John Cena shoved you inside of a coffin that was actually just a large replica of a Guns N' Roses *Use Your Illusion II* cassette tape case—yes, liner notes were included—which eventually morphed into a large replica of a freshly dug-up *E.T.* Atari video game cartridge.

— 14 —

Today you had the tastiest wet dream of all, where Slash from Guns N' Roses played a sick guitar solo on top of your bedazzled, denim-covered coffin as it was being lowered into the ground.

— 15 —

Today you tried drunkenly convincing your mom that *Goodfellas* (1990) is actually mandatory Christmastime viewing.

— 16 —

Today you giftwrapped a bunch of VHS copies of David Arquette movies you own.

— 17 —

Today, while in the mood for some real shenanigans, you used your phone to face-swap with an ALF JPEG from your "I Kill Me" desktop folder.

— 18 —

Today, while in the mood for some real shenanigans but also wanting to change things up, you used your phone to face-swap with a Jason Bateman-era *Teen Wolf* JPEG.

— 19 —

Today, while in the mood for some real shenanigans but wanting to change things up even more, you used your phone to face-swap with a piss-covered t-shirt found in a sewer drain that had "Keepin' It Real" printed on it.

— 20 —

Today you pictured yourself getting jumped and then beaten up while wearing a piss-covered sewer shirt that had "Keepin' It Real" printed on it.

— 21 —

Today you only jingled some of the way before calling an Uber.

— 22 —

Today, at the employee Christmas party, you gifted co-workers with VHS copies of David Arquette movies you once owned.

Today you tried drunkenly convincing someone that *It's a Wonderful Life* (1946) is basically the worst *Twilight Zone* episode ever.

Today, after getting black-out drunk, you giftwrapped random stuff lying around your apartment so that you'd have presents to open on Christmas morning.

Today you were genuinely surprised by the Christmas gifts you opened because you didn't remember what you'd wrapped the previous night while black-out drunk.

Today you felt bratty exhilaration in knowing that your favorite aspect of something was also the most harshly criticized by others.

Today you put holes in the wall while your neighbor was listening to the Grammy-winning 1999 hit "Smooth," but for reasons not involving Carlos Santana (or featuring Matchbox 20's Rob Thomas).

Today you tried breaking the lease on the apartment you share with the many poor decisions you've made this year.

— 29 —

Today you renamed your cat ALI: FEAR EATS THE SOUL.

— 30 —

Today you pictured yourself sitting alone on a curb in front of the corner store, slowly eating an apple-flavored Hostess pastry while crying and wearing a t-shirt with "The Dream Died" (or "Dream's Dead") (or "Dreams R.I.P.") printed on it (and it's raining).

— 31 —

Today you continued being your own therapist.

EPILOGUE

— 1 —

Today your mom called to wish you Happy New Year and then said, "Okay, I'll let you go scream into pillows or whatever it is you do."

In Memory of Mom

BONUS HOBBIES

— 1 —

Today you gave a quick shout-out to everyone listlessly going through the motions of an old dream.

Today you listened as someone complained about hiding a wad of cash "somewhere stupid," possibly in their VHS collection, which means it could be stuffed anywhere between *Meatballs* (1979) and *Spaceballs* (1987).

Today you muttered to yourself, "Respect," while acknowledging the girl at the bar who was using a pizza box as a pillow.

Today you spiritually identified with the misguided anger and solipsism of Rafael from the first Teenage Mutant Ninja Turtles film, which was streaming online for free but with ads.

Today you struggled drunkenly in a hotel room, looking for an outlet to plug your phone into while half-watching an episode of *2 Broke Girls*.

Today you contemplated the self-diagnosis of the person in a neighboring bathroom stall: "I definitely have prostate cancer."

Today you apologized to your cat for traveling to a different city, where you just sat in a strange bar, alone, listening to Ludacris sing "throw dem bows," from his 2001 hit "Southern Hospitality."

— 8 —

Today, while ignoring a football game that was on at the bar, you overheard someone say to another person, "We've got a good quarterback this year," and you said, "But do we have a good Nickelback?" but nobody acknowledged your joke, which resulted in slight disappointment.

— 9 —

Today you felt reckless from having drank three cans of Diet Dr Pepper while watching *Never Been Kissed* (1999) on a portable DVD player.

— 10 —

Today you and a co-worker were both peeing in the bathroom at work when a customer walked in and started complimenting the co-worker's *Wayne's World* hat, prompting you to say, "That's actually my hat, I just let him borrow it," which was a lie, and that's all anyone really needs to know about you as a person.

— 11 —

Today felt purposeful when Vanilla Ice's 1990 hit "Ice Ice Baby" started playing as soon as you walked into a Waffle House, but nobody noticed.

— 12 —

Today someone asked if you could help them write something nice on a Mother's Day card and you offered, "Mom, you're the bomb dot com, my love for you is humming like a CD-ROM," but they weren't impressed.

— 13 —

Today you gave a quick shout-out to the new kitchen guy who showed up on his first day wearing a t-shirt that had "Shut the fuck up, I'M COOKING" printed on it.

— 14 —

Today, when ferociously eating a banana while tweeting outside of 7-Eleven, your life momentarily felt like a movie montage where the main character struggles to accomplish their greatest feat.

— 15 —

Today you explained the plot for *Over the Top* (1987) to a stranger at the bar: "It's about a rich army brat whose mom is dying, right? And her make-a-wish is for him to bond with his deadbeat dad—played by Stallone—a truck driver moonlighting as an arm-wrestling champ. It's great. Kenny Loggins does the soundtrack."

— 16 —

Today you reminisced about a lost Polaroid from 1989, where an eight-year-old version of you is posing with the saddest guy in a Batman costume you'd ever seen while at a comic bookstore in an outlet mall on Long Island.

Today you pecked away at your *Ghostbusters: Lowlife* screenplay, which is a chilling tour de force about you and the toxicity that constantly haunts your surroundings.

Today you sent someone the *Brothers Karamazov* of texts before eventually receiving the text equivalent of an Amazon dot com sample of Snookie from MTV's *Jersey Shore*'s novel that someone haphazardly ghost wrote, which resulted in slight disappointment.

Today you cracked open your own ancient killing stone when you compulsively asked a question while knowing the answer would hurt you.

— 20 —

Today you shouted, "Alexa, why is it hard for me and others to finally accept love that doesn't taste like poison?" but Alexa didn't know.

— 21 —

Today someone, after noticing you contemplating their Grateful Dead t-shirt, asked if you were a Deadhead, and you said no, that you're more of a "grateful to actually *be* dead" type, and the person said, "Oh, so like a goth?"

— 22 —

Today you considered eating the Psilocybin mushrooms found in your sock drawer before using your ex's Hulu account to watch the Mick Foley/Antonio Sabàto Jr. episode of *Wife Swap*.

Today you bribed a homeless schizophrenic laying on the stoop in front of your apartment to leave by offering him a cigarette, which prompted him to jump up and say, "I'm queer, gimme two," so you did.

Today someone said, "I think I'm going through menopause," and you asked what menopause was, then they looked befuddled and said, "I don't actually know," and you said, "Maybe it's when you're so fed up with men that you decide to put them on pause," and they laughed, which means you now have your own Netflix stand-up comedy special in the works.

25

Today you were caught admiring the back of someone's head for a long, long time, much like one would regard a great work of art because they wore a backwards baseball cap that had the Danzig logo printed on it.

— 26 —

Today you imagined GG Allin updating his cell phone plan at a T-Mobile store and smiled.

— 27 —

Today you had to leave a bar because it was just too sad—and not just because of your own sadness, mind you; it was from having to absorb the sadness of those around you, which ultimately became too much—though luckily you found another bar where the sadness was more manageable, which was a win.

— 28 —

Today, as your soul craved a certain kind of healing, you watched the 1993 Pauly Shore film *Son in Law*, which was streaming online for free but with ads.

— 29 —

Today you stood in your kitchen, hungover and sadly eating a slice of leftover birthday cake from a party of sorority girls you'd waited on the night before.

— 30 —

Today you continued ignoring the "check engine" light that's been on inside your head for a long, long time.

— 31 —

Today, while drinking alone at the bar, you pretended that your loneliness had a rare-jewel glimmer and that maybe your hurt was shining bright like a Rihanna diamond, but if that were even true, nobody would probably notice.

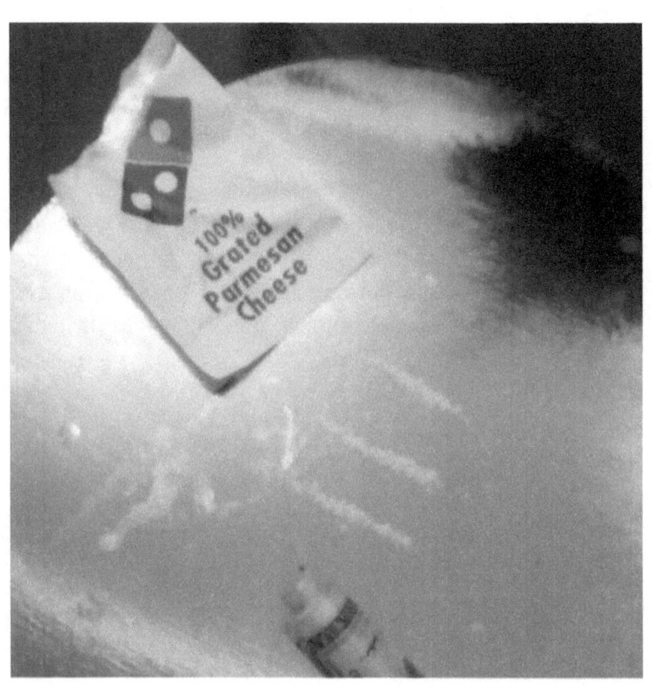
100%
Grated
Parmesan
Cheese

THE UNSEEN MESS: A REVIEW
ALANA M. KELLEY

Maudlin House
(2024)

Brian Alan Ellis's *Hobbies You Enjoy* is a darkly humorous exploration of modern ennui, capturing the absurdities of life with a raw, biting edge. As with much of Ellis's previous work, this "novelty" revels in the oddities of human existence, oscillating between moments of hilarity and despair. The title, in a lighthearted pursuit, belies the book's deeper examination of alienation, self-sabotage, and unfulfilled aspirations in modern life.

The structure of *Hobbies You Enjoy* is episodic, almost like a series of vignettes with no grand narrative arc, no sense of resolution or redemption. Instead, Ellis focuses on moments, small pockets of time that accumulate into a larger sense of existential dread. This fragmented approach reinforces the book's themes, as the protagonist moves from one aimless activity to the next.

Throughout, Ellis crafts a portrait of someone drifting through the motions of life, yearning for meaning or connection or *something* but incapable of escaping the patterns of behavior that will lead to inevitable disappointment. This tension between desire and inertia is central to the book's emotional core.

Ellis's writing is minimalist yet impactful, with a sharpness that lends itself well to both comedic and tragic moments. His style evokes the tradition of writers like Bukowski or Tao Lin, where the grit and grind of everyday life are laid bare, often with a caustic wit that punctuates the otherwise mundane. Ellis manages to extract hard truths, presenting a character who is often at their most honest when they're at their worst.

The book's cinematic dialogue presents conversations that are both hilarious and cringe-inducing, highlighting an inability to communicate effectively or to escape their social awkwardness. Ellis excels in creating these moments of tension and release, where humor is often used as a coping mechanism, masking deeper issues at play.

At the same time, Ellis doesn't shy away from the existential undertones of the story. Beneath the sarcastic, often flippant surface of the narrative, there's a palpable sense of melancholy. Hobbies and pastimes—seemingly trivial activities that one might enjoy—are, in fact, empty distractions, a way of filling the void left by unfulfilled dreams and missed opportunities. This irony is where the book finds much of its emotional weight.

Hobbies You Enjoy is a potent exploration of life's discontents. Ellis's writing is incisive, and his portrayal of human frailty is both unflinching and deeply empathetic. The book captures the absurdity of existence, balancing between comedy and tragedy, and ultimately leaves the reader with a sense of the profound loneliness that often underlies the most trivial moments of our lives. It is both a bleakly funny and melancholic commentary on the modern condition, a mirror held up to the reader, reflecting the absurdity of our own distractions, or as Ellis calls them, hobbies.

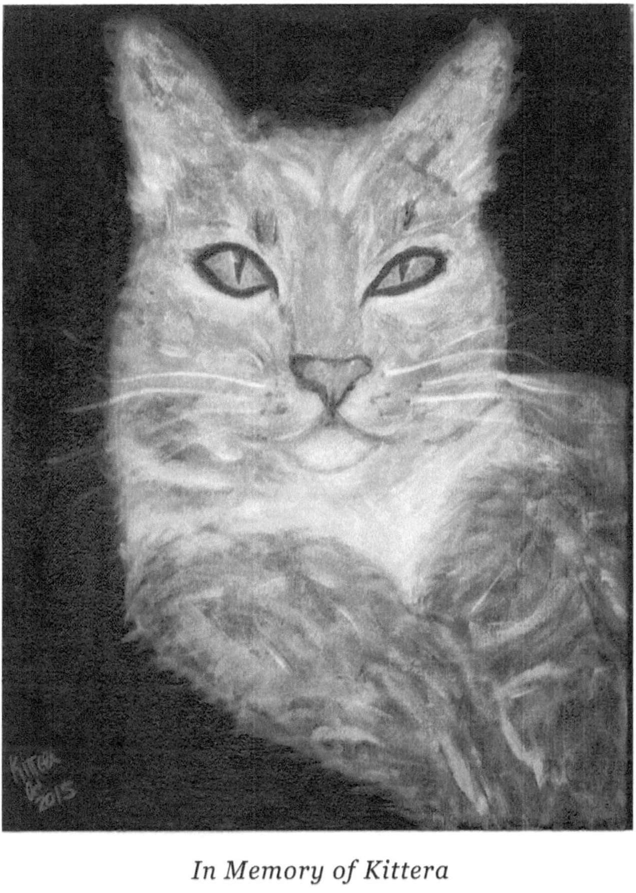

In Memory of Kittera

Want More?
Then Read...